T0116805

My Lord and My God

Seeing God in Life's Valleys

Karen Louise

WestBow
PRESS
A DIVISION OF THOMAS NELSON

Unless otherwise indicated, all references from the Bible
are to New International Version © 1984.

Scripture taken from the HOLY BIBLE, NEW INTERNATIONAL
VERSION * Copyright © 1973, 1978, 1984 Biblica. Used
by permission of Zondervan. All rights reserved.

WestBow Press books may be ordered through booksellers or by contacting:

WestBow Press
A Division of Thomas Nelson
1663 Liberty Drive
Bloomington, IN 47403
www.westbowpress.com
1-(866) 928-1240

Because of the dynamic nature of the Internet, any web addresses or links contained in this book may have changed since publication and may no longer be valid. The views expressed in this work are solely those of the author and do not necessarily reflect the views of the publisher, and the publisher hereby disclaims any responsibility for them.

Any people depicted in stock imagery provided by Thinkstock are models, and such images are being used for illustrative purposes only.
Certain stock imagery © Thinkstock.

ISBN: 978-1-4497-2886-1 (sc)
ISBN: 978-1-4497-2887-8 (hc)
ISBN: 978-1-4497-2884-7 (e)
Library of Congress Control Number: 2011918272

Printed in the United States of America

WestBow Press rev. date: 11/3/2011

Dedicated to

My Lord and My God

The older women who spoke into my life:
My mother, Erma Gingrich
Pat Clague
Ruth Laufer
May Beth Roberts

Psalm 31:7
I will be glad and rejoice in your love,
for you saw my affliction
and knew the anguish of my soul.

Acknowledgements

I would like to thank the following people for their
encouragement and support in the writing process:
My husband, Ralph for his constant support.
Dr. Miriam Adeney and Ramon Rocha for helping me start
the writing process.
Paula Bauman, Suzanne Johnson and MayBeth Roberts for
their feedback and encouragement.
Sam Wunderli (OMF) who was willing to take another risk.

Contents

Introduction

My friend, Helga, and I meandered down the cobblestone streets of a quaint Chinese town. We peeked into the colorful stalls with their various handicrafts. I stopped in front of an ornately decorated tablecloth and exclaimed in delight, "That would make a perfect gift for Debbie and Jerry." I had been a bridesmaid in their wedding party a year earlier but then had left almost immediately for a year of teaching English in China.

"Karen," Helga whispered, "there is something I must tell you."

"What?" I asked, surprised by the seriousness in her voice.

"Your mother requested that I tell you that—" Helga's voice faltered. "Debbie and Jerry were both killed in a car crash a few months ago."

I felt my legs grow weak beneath me. We both lowered ourselves to a nearby curb. "What happened?"

"Debbie was driving. It was late at night. Somehow the car veered off the road. They were both killed instantly."

My mind flashed back to three years earlier. That fall, Debbie and I had met at university in a Chinese History course. We enjoyed chatting and playing squash together but we never talked about God.

Then during first term exams, I had a dream. I saw Debbie standing at the door of heaven, expecting to enter, but the angel guarding the door denied her access. She turned and saw that I had been granted entrance. Somehow I had known the secret but had not informed her. She gazed at me with disbelief and grief, that I, her good friend, had never revealed this most important fact to her. With that, I woke up with a start, for I knew that God was trying to communicate to me through this dream.

Despite my fear that I might lose our friendship, I wrote a letter to Debbie, asking her if she would be interested in studying the Bible together. When she did not respond over the holidays, I assumed that the idea did not interest her. However, the first day back at class, she enthusiastically exclaimed that not only was she very interested but her boyfriend, Jerry, was interested in studying the Bible as well.

During that term we experienced some special times around God's word. Debbie eagerly shared with her engineering classmates her new found love of God. However, during my year in China, Debbie's letters to me included some questions. Her last letter verbalized her struggle to believe when those closest to her dismissed the reality of God.

Now, hearing of her death, I excused myself and told Helga that I just needed to be alone. I trudged outside the city walls and sat on a concrete barrier in the rice fields. "God," I cried, "where is Debbie?"

The Lord did not respond to my question. Instead He addressed my responsibility. "Karen, you did what I asked you to do. Now you must trust Debbie to me."

Although my heart mourned the loss of one of the most transparent friends I had known, in the midst of grief I knew God's peace, for God had spoken.

During these times when the world becomes dark around me, I know that I need to run to God. He holds the truth about Himself, about me, and about my situation. In His time and His way He often reveals this truth to us, if we will but wait for the revelation to come.

In this book I focus on how God reveals Himself to us during the "valley times" of our lives.

"Even though I walk through the valley of the shadow of death, I will fear no evil, for you are with me"[1] For the psalmist David, the valley included near-death experiences. Some of us can identify with him in this, some of us cannot. However, we have all passed through valley experiences or low times. During these times, the enemy often seeks to plant tiny seeds of doubt in our minds regarding the goodness and love of God. Our flesh's inclination is to guard us from these valley seasons. God, however, seems to orchestrate these times.

In the second chapter of Hosea we read these comforting words, "Therefore I am now going to allure her; I will lead her into the desert and speak tenderly to her. There I will give her back her vineyards, and will make the Valley of Achor a

---

1   Ps 23:4.

door of hope. There she will sing as in the days of her youth, as in the day she came up out of Egypt."[2] These low times sometimes hold the greatest potential for intimacy with God. During these times we can enter into a fresh understanding of who God is to us.

Although I still cringe when I embark upon an uncomfortable season, my spirit has begun to grasp the importance of embracing the season and looking for God in it.

As you view these snapshots of valleys from my life and the lives of some biblical characters, I encourage you also to look for God in your valleys. I am certain that He is there.

---

2   Hos 2:14–15.

1

My Best Friend

Have you ever had a best friend with whom you could be yourself, cry, share your dreams, and spend time with and not get bored? Well, Sue was just that kind of friend. We spent hours playing with our baby dolls and then our Barbies. Being avid readers, we would incorporate scenes from our books into our imaginary play. Once, we both stood on the edge of my family's low patio and practiced falling gracefully onto the grass, like the four sisters had in *Little Women*. We would drift off to sleep at sleepovers, telling stories to each other. Even my conversion experience at age six took place because I did not want to be separated from my best friend. Since she was going to stay after the evangelistic meeting to ask, "Jesus into her heart," so was I. Despite my faulty motives, the Holy Spirit really did enter my heart that day. Like two peas in a pod, we were inseparable from pre-kindergarten days until …

When I was in seventh grade, a new girl moved into our neighborhood. Brenda, as she was called, sat near Sue in school. The two started spending more and more time together. By the time I was in eighth grade, I no longer heard the familiar ring of the phone, with Sue's voice on the other end, asking if I would like to go out to play. Loneliness set in.

One day, as I fulfilled my chore of hanging wash on the line outside, I mulled over the situation between Sue and me. My heart ached for her companionship. Suddenly, I heard a voice say, "I am your best friend." Although I had never heard this voice before, I knew immediately Jesus had spoken. My heart leaped with gladness. From that day forward, the intense loneliness was gone. In its place was a longing to spend time with Jesus, my best friend.

The special thing about friends is that they enjoy being with each other. On Sunday afternoons, I often packed some snacks and drinks and found a quiet spot by a river with my Bible and journal. I would pour out my heart to Jesus there.

As I grew older, I would arrange "dates" with my best friend. On Valentine's Day, when I did not have a boyfriend, I would take a lighted candle and share the longings of my heart with Jesus. I always knew he listened and that he cared.

Like David, I could say, "Who on earth have I like you? In heaven there is no one besides you."[3]

One day, the freshly fallen snow glistened on the trees and the gravestones of my favorite solitary place to pray during my Wednesday lunch-hour fast. The crisp snow squeaked under my winter boots. I glanced up at a bare maple tree and saw an energetic black squirrel scurrying down the snow-laden branch. I stopped to enjoy his antics. Again, that familiar voice spoke

---

3   Ps 73:25.

into my heart. "Karen, would you take time to delight in me? Too many of my children are so busy doing things for me that they really don't enjoy me. Would you just delight in me?"

My heart warmed to his request. "Yes, Lord, yes."

During the following months and years, I tried to reserve half an hour each week during which I had no prayer agenda and no pressing needs. I would just take a walk with my best friend, as I believe Adam and Eve had done. My heart would commune with him. I would just enjoy being with him.

Now that the seasons of life have changed and the pressures of work and family have increased, I find this unhurried time with him to be less frequent. Whenever I have a chance, however, I still try to take walks with my best friend and just enjoy being with him.

***

The young man fixed his gaze straight ahead, eager for the sight of the place he now called home. He and his men had trudged three days over desert terrain. Discouragement tugged at their hearts. They had left their homes full of zeal, ready to fight in battle, only to be denied that privilege by army commanders.

Passing the familiar sycamore tree near their town, the young warrior and his troops hurried their steps. Within minutes, they would be reunited with their loved ones. They rounded the final rocky crest. Suddenly, their footsteps halted. Their mouths gaped, their eyes bulged, and cries from deep within their hearts exploded. Then, as if one man, they raced to where their homes once had been. Nothing but ashes and lingering wisps of smoke remained. Raiding bands had carried off their loved ones.

These huge, muscular men threw themselves on the mound that had once been their lodgings. Loud wailing resounded throughout the remains of the smoking town. The men wept until they had no strength left to weep.[4] Then, their grief turned to anger. Gathering together, they conspired to stone their once-respected leader.

Their young leader overheard their plans. His heart was rent. His two beloved wives had been taken captive. Now, his men, who had stood with him against the attacks of his country's mad king, were prepared to kill him. Despair threatened to engulf him. Then he made a choice. He looked up. He looked up to the God who had been with him since infancy. He looked up to the God who had saved him from the lion and the bear. He looked up to the God who had helped him kill Goliath. He looked up to the God who had delivered him from the sword of Saul. He looked up to the God who had become his best friend throughout life, and he found strength in the Lord his God, in the friend who would never leave or forsake him. He found solace in his best friend's presence.

Read: 1 Samuel 29:1–30:6

———◆———

A Best Friend:
Someone who comes in when everyone
else goes out.

———◆———

---

4   1Sam 30:4.

2

My Way

The environment in the cramped living room of that noisy downtown apartment disturbed me. I felt like a cockroach that was suddenly exposed by a bright light. I had no place to run and hide from the penetrating light. Yet, a presence inside me whispered that I, too, belonged to the light. *Then why,* I questioned myself, *do I feel so uneasy under the hospitality of these two godly German women, who live their faith more than just verbalize it?*

Only a week before, I had arrived in Hong Kong, en route to Beijing. Although as a child I had already recognized that God had called me to be his ambassador to the nations, at this stage of my life, I deeply resented being labeled a "missionary."

How could I encourage people to deny themselves and follow Christ alone, when I entertained the idea that there may be many ways to God? Was not love all that was really needed to make this world a better place? How dare missionaries propound the idea that other beliefs were wrong, when their own lives sometimes lacked a sincere love for their fellow man?

As my visit in Hong Kong drew to a close, the controversy raging within my heart erupted. I poured out my confused thoughts to my older hostess. She patiently listened. Then, looking me in the eyes, she asked, "If there was another way for the world to be saved, why did Jesus have to die?"

Instantly, light shone into my heart, dispelling the darkness. How could a loving Father allow His only son to die, if there was another way to salvation? I knew that Jesus was the only way.

My friend continued, "You are at the crossroads between the narrow way and the wide way. If you choose the narrow way, some of your friends, including some Christian friends, may perceive you as being narrow-minded and resent you. Are you prepared for that?"

The enlightenment had come, however. I knew that I must be faithful to truth revealed. I braced myself for the rejection of some of my friends and declared to the unseen world that I would walk the narrow road.

That choice led to an acceleration of discoveries about God, myself, and the world around me. Spiritual truths could not be gleaned through the intellect alone; they depended upon the gracious work of the Spirit of Truth. Each week He seemed to teach me a new lesson. Often at the beginning of a new month I would prayerfully ask Him what the focus of that month's lessons would be. Boredom with life fled, as I had Truth as my teacher by my side.

"These followers of the way must be stopped. They are turning the world of Judaism upside down. How dare they proclaim that this man Jesus is superior to our forefathers! The traditions of Judaism were handed down by Moses himself. It is sacrilegious to proclaim another gospel other than the one of the past."

This Pharisee's zeal consumed him. "I am willing to be responsible for their deaths. Give me a legal search warrant and I will hunt them down on the highways and byways." Those listening nodded their approval. Death was the only way to stop this new sect from spreading. Its teachings had already in-filtrated many of their families. Wives, children, and more distant relatives had been brainwashed into believing its false claims—all surrounding a dead man.

Feeling justified in their course of action, the group dispersed. Many promised to accompany the confident rabbi to Damascus on the first day of the following week.

Sunday arrived. Search warrant tucked into the inside of his flowing robe, the religious leader led the excited mob down the dusty road toward Damascus. Which best suited these fanatics: death by crucifixion, the sword, the gladiators, the wild animals, or stoning? The people chuckled as they threw out their opinions in Aramaic.

Observers could easily have mistaken the noisy throng as enthusiastic, bloodthirsty Romans heading for the coliseum had it not been for the prayer caps and tassels which distinguished them as Jewish religious leaders.

Excitement mounted as they neared Damascus. Suddenly a light from heaven flashed around the young leader. He fell to the ground. A voice said to him, "Why do you persecute me?"

In confusion the man replied, "Who are you, Lord?"

"I am Jesus, whom you are persecuting. Now get up and go to the city and you will be told what you must do."

His fellow travelers stood speechless. They heard the sound but did not see anyone.[5]

When the rabbi rose from the ground he opened his eyes, but all was as night around him. He could not see. In unaccustomed humility he requested that his friends lead him into Damascus.

For three days he remained isolated in a room, not desiring the voices of his friends or food and drink. His thoughts were his sole companions.

He faced what the revelation on the road meant to him. He had been wrong. Jesus was alive. His teachings lived on through the followers of the Way. Now what did this mean to his future? He could not continue his life as he had lived it before. He was knowledgeable of the teaching of Jesus' followers. They insisted that salvation could not be earned through the law of Moses; it could only be obtained through faith in Jesus. If he embraced this teaching, he must turn his back on his traditions, his family, and his society. If he refused to accept Jesus after this revelation, he would have to live the rest of his life as a lie, going through the motions of a tradition that no longer held hope for eternal life. He himself would be most miserable.

Was he willing to follow Jesus as the only way the rest of his life, regardless of the cost?

---

5   Ac 9:4–7.

In his inner being, he felt he had no choice. He had seen the light. He must now walk in that light.

In the midst of these thoughts he heard a knock. He stumbled to open the door to the voice of a man he did not recognize. What would the future hold for him?

Read: Acts 9:1–19

———✦◈✦———

The Way:
The only road which will enable you to reach
your destination.

———✦◈✦———

3

My Deliverer

I tossed and turned on my narrow cot. Sleep and peace eluded me. The words of Romans 8:6 pricked my consciousness. "The mind of sinful man is death, but the mind controlled by the Spirit is life and peace." How I longed for that peace and life. For two weeks now, I had experienced what I labeled the "torment of my soul." I sometimes thought physical death would be easier than this constant raging of the soul. How I longed to be free. But try as I might, I could not find release from my sin.

For many years I had quite enjoyed the attention of different men. My ego feasted on it. But now, as I caught a glimpse of my true condition, I realized I was addicted to this attention. I could not be content without my ego being fed this kind of affirmation from a man. This attention, which once gave me a feeling of self-worth, now seemed to be sucking from me my self-respect. I began to hate myself.

However, I consoled myself with the thought that I would soon be in Hong Kong for the Spring Festival. Once I left Beijing, where I had been teaching for the past term, I would be free of this torment. I would be free of this habit. Little did I know that the root of this habit was a part of me and would follow me wherever I went.

With relief I crawled in between the crisp, clean sheets of my bed in Hong Kong and slipped into the first deep sleep I had had in a long time. However, within a week that same nasty habit reared its ugly head. Would I never have freedom?

My hostess, the same godly German woman who had spoken into my life before, pulled me aside one day. "Karen, I have a question I must ask you. You have been a believer for so many years. Why is it that you still have not grown much in maturity in the Lord?"

I was stumped. I really did not know.

My friend challenged me. "I want you to go away and pray. Ask the Lord why this is so. Then we will talk again."

The next day, I questioned the Lord, but the heavens seemed as brass. I had no answer.

When my friend and I again met, she shared how the Lord had shown her a picture of me. It was not a nice picture. In the picture she had seen a dark, hooded figure pushing me up a hill.

When I asked what this figure was, she gave a one-word reply: "Lust."

My tears started to flow. My body was racked with sobs. I knew she had spoken the truth. This is what kept me in bondage.

She lifted my chin and looked me in the eyes. "Karen, do you want to be free?"

"Yes, yes," I sniffled.

"Karen, if I pray for you, I need to know that you are willing to change, that you really do not want to lead this kind of life anymore."

Without hesitation I gave her my assurance.

Then she prayed. It was a simple prayer. All I remember is that for almost half an hour the tears did not stop flowing. When finally my body became quiet, my heart was filled with peace. I knew I was free! Jesus had delivered me.

As dusk closed in upon the city, she hurried past the city gates to the outskirts of the town. She knew what was expected of her. She knew the ability within her. Some said she had an invisible magnet which lured unguarded men to follow her to the room she had prepared for them. She was uncanny. Even well-intentioned husbands and good fathers felt themselves being drawn into her embrace. The women of the town hated her. How many of their husbands had been unfaithful to them on account of her? The men of the town despised her for what she did to their reputation and families, and yet there was something about her which they found attractive and irresistible.

One day a new man appeared on the scene. The town was in a frenzy about his coming. Some said that he had the power to heal the sick. Some said that he was the promised Messiah. She felt the need for neither a healer nor a messiah. Out of curiosity, however, she followed the crowds.

As she came within sight of the healer, something churned within her. Clutching her stomach, she sat down on a stone at the edge of the swarming crowd. There was something about this man which instilled fear in her. She knew he had the ability to radically change her life. She was not prepared for that. She resolved to stay hidden.

Suddenly she heard her name; someone was calling her to come.

An old woman nearby jabbed her on the shoulder, "He's calling you, scoundrel, you'd better move it."

The woman did not know if she should run or yield. A power greater than the forces within seemed to be drawing her forward. As she pushed her way through the crowd, she fell down before Him. Her hair brushed His feet. He took her by the hand and helped her up. The crowd gasped. Did He know who He was touching?

Looking into her eyes, the man asked, "Do you want to be free?"

Suddenly from deep within her being she did want to be free. In this man's presence she felt so dirty, so unclean. All of a sudden she longed to be clean, to be whole. "Yes Lord, yes!" she exclaimed.

Then he gave a simple command to the spirits and they fled with a screech. The crowd counted as they sensed them leave. "One, two, three, four, five, six, seven." All became quiet. Everyone knew that the town would be different from that day forward. The town's whore had been set free.

For the first time in her life, the woman did not want to draw attention to herself. With a whispered thank-you to the man who had delivered her, she weaved her way back to the edges of the crowd. Dropping onto that same stone, she poured out her gratefulness to her God for ordaining this day for her deliverance. She resolved that she would follow the Messiah who had set her free for the rest of the days of her life.

Read: Luke 8:1–3, John 19:25–27, Matthew 27:57–61, John 20:1–18

———◆———

The Deliverer:
The one who is able to free you from that which you cannot free yourself.

———◆———

4

My Covering

The first rays of light peeked through the faded, dismal curtains that hung from my crowded living room, and trickled into my adjoining bedroom. With eagerness I sat up and swung my feet to the cold concrete floor. Tucking my feet into my warm, fuzzy slippers, I rushed to the kitchen sink and splashed my face with the refreshing coolness of the water. This time I did not complain that my tiny flat had no hot water. Relieved that the restless night was behind me, I pulled a worn string and the room's single light bulb flooded the room with brightness. Reaching for my Bible as one reaches for a letter from a dear friend, I sat down in the only soft chair in the room. My Bible fell open to the verses which had echoed in my mind since the early morning hours: "When I want to do good, evil is right there with me. For in my inner being I delight in God's law, but I see another law at work in the members of my body, waging war against the law of my mind and making me a prisoner of the law of sin at work within my members. What a wretched [woman] I am! Who will rescue me from this body of death?"[6]

I took comfort that others in this world struggled against sin and sometimes felt that pull to the side of defeat rather than toward victory. However, was this the position I had to remain in? Was life a continual struggle against the sins of the flesh and especially against those besetting sins?

My eyes skipped ahead to the next chapter: "There is now no condemnation for those who are in Christ Jesus."[7] Was I in Christ Jesus?

Yes, I was. Then why did I still feel condemned?

I read on. "Because through Christ Jesus ... who became a sin offering ... the law of the Spirit of life set me free from the law of sin and death."[8] There was hope! I raised my face heavenward. "Please, Lord," I pleaded, "set me free from this mind and body of death!"

Then suddenly before me I saw a picture. I stood inside a door frame. God's wrath was approaching. I trembled, knowing what it meant. Then Jesus appeared at my side and placed His blood over the door. Looking up at God in His wrath, Jesus defended me. "Pass her by, for she is covered by My blood."

I crumbled to my knees in gratitude as I saw God's wrath pass me by. I knew that without the blood of Jesus, I was dead. His blood and finished work on the cross provided me with hope and freedom. There was no condemnation but rather life for me! I could know victory on this side of the grave from the besetting sins of my life.

---

6   Ro 7:21–24
7   Ro 8:1
8   Ro 8:2, 3

Later as a married woman and mother a situation happened in our family which demonstrated the power of the blood. We had left our ministry in Asia for a nine month home assignment. During that time, the Lord impressed upon me to meditate on the power of the blood of Jesus.

While we were back in Canada , our oldest son Daniel, who was eight years old at the time, had saved all his money to buy a dog when we returned to Asia. Shortly after arriving back in Asia, we made the eight-hour bus journey to the nearest big city to choose the perfect dog. Daniel finally settled on a brown-haired male golden retriever puppy he named Maple. With pride he carried the little box that contained his pup all the way back home on the windy bus ride. For the next week laughter sounded within the walls of our house as Daniel and his two younger brothers enjoyed watching the newest addition to the family chase his tail and catch balls.

On the eighth day, however, we watched in dismay as our once energetic pup refused to eat or play. Instead, Maple grew weaker and sicker. We took him to a vet, who gave him an intravenous treatment for five hours a day. But he did not respond to the treatment. We went to bed at night wondering if Maple would still be alive the next morning.

Finally one morning, when Maple and I arrived at the vet's for his treatment, a big German shepherd dog greeted us. After securing Maple's tiny paws to the table, the vet instructed the huge dog to jump up on an adjacent table. While the dog lay there calmly, the vet withdrew a large syringe of blood. Then he injected the needle into our puppy's frail body and gave him a little blood as a test. When half an hour passed and Maple showed no allergic reaction, the vet proceeded to give him the remainder of the blood. Within a few hours, we all knew that

Maple no longer lingered at death's door and that his life was restored. The big dog's blood had provided him with life. The natural immunities which the German shepherd had acquired to fight the same disease our pup had, now enabled Maple to resist the disease as well. Without the aid of the other dog's blood, Maple would have died.

I thanked God not only for saving Maple but for giving me a tangible example of the power of Jesus' blood to overcome disease, sin and death.

Through a strange set of circumstances the two boys had become friends. One lived in Goshen and the other lived in the courts of the Great Pharaoh. Whenever the young lad from Goshen could steal away from his tedious work of mixing mortar, he would run through the secret passageway he had been shown and enter the beautiful orchard of Pharaoh. Then he would ring a little bell that signaled to his friend to come out to play.

When his young Egyptian friend appeared, the two of them would do what most ordinary boys do. They would run down to the little stream and build rock dams, or they would make little boats out of papyrus leaves. Sometimes they would persuade the cook to give them some tasty stew of leeks and eggplant, sautéed with garlic. Regardless of what their hands found to do, the boys constantly chatted, sharing with each other their fears and frustrations and their hopes and dreams. No one would have guessed that different cultures separated them or that their families' different choices of beliefs would separate them for eternity.

Then one day, the young Hebrew boy from Goshen was not allowed to leave his house. His father warned him that only upon risk of death could he leave the house that evening. He must join his family and assist in killing a one-year-old lamb, then he must follow his father's example and paint the doorposts of the house with the lamb's blood. That night they would all eat a meal of roasted mutton and flat bread made without yeast. They were to prepare all their belongings, for God had promised that they were to leave the next day.

The young Hebrew lad could sense the mounting excitement in Goshen, because for years the people had cried out to God to deliver them from the Egyptians. His own heart, however, carried mixed emotions. On one hand, he, like all his people, longed for a new beginning, longed for the Promised Land. On the other hand, he had never had such a good friend as the young Egyptian son of royalty. Surely, he could not go without saying goodbye.

As his family prepared to lie down for a few hours of sleep, he mentally planned his exit strategy. He lay there in the dark, waiting for his father to fall asleep. His father however, seemed to be fighting the usually welcomed friend of sleep. He seemed to be on guard. What was he on guard for?

Then all of a sudden he felt it. It was an awesome, fearful, powerful presence. It seemed to sweep over the entire house— and then it was gone. It left him feeling chilled, stripped of all his defenses, and exposed in heart. He turned his eyes away from the door. Gone was his desire to go outside. He clung to the safety of his home.

Moments—or was it hours?—passed. He lay in the darkness, unable to sleep. Suddenly a shrill cry went up, then another. Soon the night air was filled with the sound of wailing—

wailing as one wails at a funeral. Feet could be heard running on the road outside. "Go! Go! Go, you cursed Israelites! The Pharaoh has commanded you to go. Even his own son lies dead at his feet. Go now!"

As if this were the cue his father had been waiting for, his father awakened his sleeping family. Quickly he ushered them into the cool night air to the prepared donkeys and camels. The boy, however, struggled to move. Again the news carried with it a double edge. Yes, the day they had awaited was finally here, but ... sobs swelled up from within him. His friend was dead. His dear, dear friend was dead. He himself was saved, all because of the blood.

"Oh, God!" he cried, "Could not your blood have saved the Egyptians, too?"

Deep within his heart came a reply, "Yes, my son, if they had availed themselves of the blood, they too could have been saved."

Perhaps he alone of the Hebrews found himself crying for the Egyptians, "God, please send people to them in the future to let them know the power that is in the blood to save them from your wrath. Only your blood can truly cover them."

Read: Exodus 11:1-12:42

---◆---

A Covering:
That protective layer which separates us from undesirable
elements, punishments, or curses.

---◆---

5

My Counselor

When a heart needs unpacking, God often chooses His trusted
servants to be His hands and feet on this earth. His hands and
feet in the season of my heart's unpacking came in the form of
a missionary named Ruth.

Ruth, a spry older German lady, lived what she taught.
For many years she and her co-worker had faithfully served
the Indonesian children in Asia. Then, at an age when many
workers her age were returning to the comforts of their native
country, God gave Ruth and her co-worker a fresh vision,
a new country, and a new language. Believing that God is
faithful to provide all that we need to fulfill the vision He gives
us, she and her co-worker responded in faith. So it happened
that God allowed our paths to cross in the hustle and bustle of
Hong Kong.

For a year she faithfully prayed and spoke into my life.
Branches which bore no fruit were cut away and those which

did bear fruit were pruned. The expectation grew within me that when I met with Ruth, I would also have an encounter with God.

So, in anticipation, I looked forward to meeting with Ruth in Germany en route to Canada.

As Hilda, my German hostess, and I climbed the narrow passage up to Ruth's cozy little apartment on the second floor, my eyes glowed with the anticipation of having a heart-to-heart chat. However, after we were introduced and welcomed, and as time dwindled away and the topics of conversation between the three of us failed to turn to deeper things, fear started to rise within me. What would I do without Ruth's counsel in my life? I had come to expect God to use Ruth as a channel to speak into my life. Now my one hope to hear God speak into the inner workings of my heart seemed to be vanishing.

As we stood up from the table and slowly made our way down the dark stairway, my heart cried. "Lord, how could I face the future without Ruth?" I did not know when our paths would cross again.

Then into my heart came the Lord's soft but firm voice. "Karen, I have used Ruth in your life for this season. From here on, you will depend on no one as you depended upon Ruth. You must hold lightly to relationships. I will bring people into your life but I will also take them away. I am the one that you must lean on. I will be your Counselor and guide you in paths of all truth."

As we embraced and exchanged goodbyes at the train station, I knew that a chapter of my life had closed, but I also knew that God would lead me on. He would counsel me. He would always be there for me.

I thank God for His servants and how He has used them in my life, but I know that I can never count on them to always be there for me. That position belongs to God alone. He is jealous for His rightful position.

God is faithful. For the next two years of my life, almost daily tears accompanied my times alone with God. As I would pour out to Him the fears and anxiety of my heart, He would reveal the root. Often it lay in a sinful thought pattern. In His graciousness, He would bring His truth to bear on the situation. He would also show me who He was and who I was to Him in that situation. Then peace would come into my heart. I began to become convinced that no sin was too great, no stronghold too strong, no situation too hopeless for Him to break in and bring His light and freedom. He indeed is the world's best Counselor for He made the heart and understands the heart. Nothing can hide from His gaze.

The chilly night air encouraged the men to huddle closely together round the fire in their room. Their ears bent close to hear every word that their beloved teacher was saying. The tone behind His words at times sent fear creeping through their souls. He seemed to be giving a farewell speech instead of a Passover teaching.

"If the world hates you, keep in mind that it hated me first. If you belonged to the world, it would love you as its own. As it is, you do not belong to the world, but I have chosen you out of the world. That is why the world hates you."[9]

9   Jn 15:18,19.

As the men listened to their teacher's words, the gulf between them and those who rejected their master widened. They would never be part of "normal" society now. They were different. They followed a different drummer.

"I certainly hope He stays with us to give us the needed strength, courage, and direction," one of the men whispered to his neighbor. "Without Him beside me, I would be lost and in despair."

As if hearing the whispered words, the teacher stated, "Because I have said these things, you are filled with grief. But I tell you the truth: it is for your good that I am going away."[10]

"How could any good come from Him leaving us?" a burly fisherman muttered under his breath.

"I tell you the truth: it is for your good that I am going away."[11]

"Doesn't He know how much we need Him?" A man with a thick Galilean accent nudged the man next to him.

The teacher continued. His eyes seemed to penetrate into their souls and remove all further questions from their thoughts. "Unless I go away, the Counselor will not come to you; but if I go, I will send Him to you."[12]

The teacher's eyes got moist with tears. His voice choked with emotion. "I have much more to say to you, more than you can now bear. But when He, the Spirit of Truth, comes, He will guide you into all truth. He will not speak on His own: He will speak only what He hears, and He will tell you what is yet to come. He will bring glory to me by taking from what is mine and making it known to you."[13]

---

10 Jn 16:6.
11 Jn 16:7
12 Jn 16:7
13 Jn 16:12–14

The men eyed each other, "Spirit of all truth?" They were accustomed to their teacher being by their side. How could the spirit speak with such clarity as their Lord?

Their master, as if knowing their thoughts, continued, "The Spirit will take from me what is mine and make it known to you."

"Make it known to you?" The men at the back discussed among themselves what this could mean. Surely, they finally concluded, the Spirit of Truth would speak with the same clarity of Jesus and understanding would be given them. Now their hearts dared, just a little, to look past the grief which their teacher had just described, to the promise of one who would come to guide them into all truth. They would not be left as orphans when their teacher left. They would have another who would never leave them and who could be all places at once, for He is spirit. Although their minds could not fully comprehend all that the teacher said, the fear that had stolen into their hearts seemed to be replaced by a supernatural peace. Everything would be all right.

Read: John 16:5–16

⟫◈⟪

The Counselor:
The one who is familiar with the inner workings of the heart and who is able to unravel them when they get tangled.

⟫◈⟪

27

6

My Joy Giver

Brushing back tears, I raced back and forth on the flat rooftop of the compound which imprisoned me. Where was God? The tension which built up daily within me found only one release. That occurred in my evening runs on the rooftop.

Although I had no doubt that God had called me to this mid-Saharan desert place, yet I had expected to feel His presence, to know His guidance. Now when I cried out to Him, all was silent.

My days were consumed with writing English material for a private English and computer training center. Given the strictures of the Muslim community I resided in and the lack of law in the city, as a woman I was not permitted outside the compound alone. I lived, taught, and slept in the three-story concrete building.

One day as I cried my heart out to God, He finally answered me.

"Karen, wait for me.

I will again show myself to you.

It will be different than before.

Wait for me and you will yet see me."

"Wait." The word was "wait." My fingers flipped through the Bible, looking up many references that contained the word wait. The abundance of them surprised me. I was not the only one that God had confined to a waiting room.

Then one day it happened. Sitting in my sparsely furnished bedroom, which contained only a mattress on the floor and a cardboard box for a wardrobe, I put on a worship tape. As I started to sing along with the music, suddenly the Holy Spirit caught hold of me. I found myself in the middle of that near-empty room dancing with all my might, just as David may have danced by the ark. Having been raised in a conservative Christian home, dancing as an expression of worship was not part of my experience. I knew that the Holy Spirit had taken hold of me. After an hour of worshiping my God through dance, my heart seemed again joined to His. I raced downstairs. My face gleamed not only from the mid-afternoon Saharan heat but from the joy of having found God's heart again. Desiring someone to share my joy with, I sought out my teaching companion. Stumbling over words, I attempted to express what had just happened.

"That's nice," he responded politely, without much more than a quick glance over his Arabic textbook.

I slipped away. I realized he could not comprehend my joy because it was something very personal between my Lord and myself.

I ran back upstairs to my little sanctuary and poured out my heart in thanksgiving to my Abba Father for the tangible expression of His presence to me. My confidence soared. If God could meet me in such a dry, barren place as this, He could meet me anywhere, anytime. I did not need to fear that He would not be there for me in the future. He would surely always meet me, in the good times and in the bad. He was my joy!

The older man shifted his gaze from one to the other of the men who surrounded him. His heart filled with despair. No chance remained that they would alter their plans. His days were surely numbered.

Then they grabbed him and tied his hands with ropes. Attaching a long, worn rope to the bonds which secured his hands, they pushed him into the king's son's cistern. They laughed as he dangled in mid-air. Slowly, slowly, they lowered him into the slimy mud which oozed thickly at the bottom of the waterless well. The coolness of the wet, murky earth offered some minor relief to his raw, open sores—reminders of his recent imprisonment. However, as the mud reached his thighs, then his hips, he cried out to God. "God, God, where are you?"

The promises the Lord had made when he first began his ministry flashed across his traumatized mind: "They will fight against you but will not overcome you, for I am with you and will rescue you."[14]

Suddenly, despite the mire, the turmoil in his mind ceased. He would be saved. How, he did not know, but he would be saved. His God had promised.

---

14   Jer 1:19.

Then as he felt the mud reach his chest, it was almost as if his heart heard a voice say to the hordes of darkness around him, "This far and no more; the boundary line is drawn."

He heaved a sigh of relief. He knew that the darkness could do no more than God Almighty allowed.

His body aching, he tried to find some position that would allow for sleep. As he was about to drift off to sleep, he sensed his Almighty God's arms around him, not only sustaining him but placing his feet upon solid rock. The weariness which had been his constant companion over the past season of imprisonment left him and he was filled with an unspeakable joy. His mouth wanted to shout his Creator's praise. He laughed in spite of his situation. Even a pit could not keep His God's joy from him. Life was still worth living. With this thought he drifted into a peaceful sleep.

The next morning, just after sunrise, he heard voices around the cistern. He recognized the voice of a dark-skinned supporter, a Cushite who held an official position in the royal palace. The familiar voice shouted, "Take these rags we're lowering down. Put them under your armpits. Secure the ropes around you. We will lift you out."

In relief for God's provision of salvation, the weak and hungry man quickly obeyed. Slowly, painfully, the man was lifted to freedom. His eyes blinked as they came into contact with the brightness of the morning sun. With his ropes cut, he threw his arms open wide in gratitude. "Father God, thank you that in you I am always free, whether in chains or without, for your joy knows no bonds." With that, he sank to his knees, too exhausted to stand.

The Cushite quickly rushed over and helped him to a comfortable shady spot. "Wait here," he instructed," while I go and find some bread and water for you."

The older man nodded and settled down to enjoy the external freedom which mirrored the inner freedom he had experienced the night before.

Read: Jeremiah 38

—⟫◆⟪—

The Joy Giver:
The one who is able to bring joy
when we are in the pit.

—⟫◆⟪—

7

My Restorer

The clarity of the call remained undeniable. What had happened? How had I allowed the enemy to cause me to stumble once again? I mentally recalled the past year.

After returning from Asia, I had a clear impression that I needed to fast regularly and pray for a North African country. Three months later, out of the blue, a friend's father's friend had telephoned, wondering if I would be interested in teaching in the country I had been praying for. From that time I had casually started praying about the possibility. When two months later the man called again, demanding a definite answer within a week, I got down on my knees and earnestly sought God. God drew my attention to Luke 10:3. "I am sending you like lambs among wolves." Not wanting to be presumptuous, I asked God for confirmation. That week at church the speaker shared from that same passage. In faith, I proceeded forward. Two months later I found myself in the middle of the Sahara at a little Computer-English Training Center. Knowing God had called me to pray, I devoted my noon siestas to prayer.

Then on a day that had started like all the others, everything changed. A young Arab man from one of the desert tribes entered the center. His gentle, caring manners stood in stark contrast to the harsh environment which surrounded me. He possessed the ancient art of poetic verse and spoke fluent English. Perhaps it was loneliness, or perhaps it was isolation from the English-speaking world, or perhaps it was—well, whatever it was, my heart no longer sought after my Father's will but instead sought the affection of a man.

A couple of months later, as the plane touched down on Canadian soil, tears covered the surface of my heart. The tears stemmed in small part from having said goodbye to a man who had found his way into my life, but more from knowing that I had departed from my Father's heart and will. How could I ever look God in the face again, knowing that I had again chosen a man's affirmation over the security which only He could give? In the process, I had failed to honor His name in the country to which He had called me.

Returning to church and my family, I felt distant and unable to connect. For the next five months, I went through the motions of living and believing. I had brought the wilderness back home with me. Even more challenging than the cultural readjustment to life in North America was the failure that was hidden in my heart. I could tell no one. I had disappointed others, myself, and God.

When a friend invited me to go with her husband and her to a large Christian meeting, I politely accepted. At the beginning of the service she turned to me and asked, "Are you expecting to receive anything tonight?"

I honestly acknowledged to myself that I was not expecting anything from God. Then I found myself crying out to Him to change my heart again so I would again be able to come before Him with expectancy.

When the altar call was given at the end of the service, I made my way to the front. I have no recollection of anyone praying for me, but Jesus met me there. In my mind I saw Jesus standing in a meadow with beautiful wildflowers. People gathered around him. He beckoned for me to come, but I shied away. I did not go. Then He approached me. He spoke my name. As soon as I heard my name on His lips I turned to His embrace. He held me as I sobbed. I knew that He had forgiven me again. I knew that I was still His child.

A few weeks later, I headed out the door to visit my cousin.

"He may not recognize you for he is often quite confused," my mother warned, hoping I would not be disappointed.

My cousin Ron had struggled with homosexuality for much of his life. He was now dying of AIDS. Although Ron was more than ten years my senior, we had always shared a quiet understanding of each other. I appreciated his thoughtful questions, his consideration for others, and his love of nature. Now I felt the Lord's prompting to go and visit him.

When I entered the door of my relatives' home, Ron immediately looked up and asked, "How was Libya?" His thinking was amazingly clear that day.

I answered as best I could. I recounted how I had sinned and the distance that it had created between God and me. I shared with him the picture in the garden which the Lord had given. Then Ron gazed at me with his penetrating eyes. "Why were you afraid to go to Him?" he whispered.

"I felt unworthy. I felt like I had failed God."

Ron's body started to tremble with sobs. I put my arms around his frail body and held him close as he wept. When his tears subsided, he whispered, "I want to go to Jesus. Would you pray for me?"

With tearful eyes, the two of us lifted up our hearts to His throne of mercy.

As I left that day, I doubted if I would ever see Ron alive again, but I knew the angels were rejoicing in heaven and that one day I would see Ron there.

The bearded fisherman shifted his gaze from the empty nets to the shore. Was that a lone fisherman walking there?

The figure, catching the fisherman's gaze, shouted, "Friends, haven't you any fish?"[15]

"No," the weary men in the boat yelled in return.

Then as if all authority were His, the stranger on the shore instructed, "Throw your net on the other side of the boat and you will find some."[16]

The men were rewarded for their obedience. The net was bursting with fish.

Suddenly the bearded man recognized who that lone figure was. It was the Lord! Tucking his outer garment around him, he jumped into the chilly, early morning waters. He desperately desired to know that Jesus accepted him. For the past days his

15   Jn 21:5.
16   Jn 21:6.

guilt had weighed him down. Sometimes at night he would wake up in a cold sweat, seeing his master's piercing eyes looking through the windows of his soul into the depths of his heart at the time the rooster crowed. How could he ever have denied the Son of God? How could he ever have said that he did not know his best friend?

As he trudged up to shore, he saw that the Lord had already started a fire. However, seeing his friends struggling to pull in the boat laden with fish, he sighed; his confession would need to wait. He dutifully assisted the others in bringing in the huge catch.

After breakfast, before he even had a chance to pour out his heart to the Lord, his master turned to him and asked, "Do you truly love me more than these?"[17]

"You know that I love you," the burly fisherman blurted out.

"Feed my lambs."

The man's heart gladdened. His master still considered him worthy enough to feed the little ones.

The Lord reiterated: "Do you truly love me?"

The fisherman answered in the affirmative, puzzled that He would ask him again.

"Take care of my sheep."

"Oh," thought the bearded man. "He is still willing to entrust me with the needs of his sheep."

Jesus' voice continued to be heard above the sound of the waves. "Do you love me?"

Feeling a little hurt that the Lord should still doubt his love, the fisherman emphatically spoke. "Lord, you know all things; you know that I love you."

17   Jn 21:15.

This time Jesus answered, "Feed my sheep."[18]

The man's heart rose. The Lord was restoring him back to the full responsibilities He had given him before. His heart leapt for joy. His master had truly forgiven him and saw him not as his failure depicted him but through the eyes of love's hope. The Lord was willing to entrust His sheep to him again in all aspects, not just in part. Oh, how he yearned to be found faithful to his Lord this time until the day he died.

Read: John 21: 1-17

The Restorer:
The one who has the ability to restore inner peace and expectancy to the heart and bring healing to broken relationships.

---

18   Jn 21:15–17.

8

My All-Sufficiency

"But Lord," I begged, "I would prefer to go to Thailand rather than South Korea."

The Lord would not budge. The four countries remained the same: South Korea, China, Mongolia, and Hong Kong.

In obedience I purchased a plane ticket to Asia, not knowing exactly what was in store for me. All through my Asian prayer journey that August, however, I experienced my Lord's gracious hand upon me.

As I sat on the plane from Beijing to Mongolia, I asked the Lord why He wanted me to go to there. I knew no one in that northern country.

"Children," came His only response.

When I disembarked from the plane, a young woman from the travel company I had contacted greeted me. She led me to a jeep and together we rode over the rugged terrain to Ulaanbaatar, the capital city of Mongolia.

When we finally arrived at the travel office, the tall South African manager extended his hand in welcome. He questioned me regarding my purposes and asked about my expectations. Something he said hinted that he, too, Was a believer; so sinking into the hard wooden chair in his spacious office, I disclosed why I believed God had sent me to Mongolia.

A broad smile spread across his face. "We have an American woman here who has a ministry to street children. I will call her and arrange for you to see her before you go to your hotel."

A short time later, I found myself knocking at a heavy door. Quick footsteps could be heard inside. When the door swung open, a petite gray-haired woman greeted me. Beckoning me to come into her simple abode, she stepped aside to allow me to enter with my bulky luggage.

"Where are you from?" she asked, helping me remove my heavy backpack.

"From Toronto, Canada."

The hostess gasped. "Toronto! I was on my knees all morning asking God to send me someone from Toronto, and now here you are."

Her hands reached for a ring of keys hanging from a hook on the wall. "Please stay here this week," she requested, laying the keys in my hand.

Through situations like this I saw God lead me in an amazing way through my journey across Asia—until I landed in Hong Kong.

When I arrived in Hong Kong I searched the waiting crowd for the familiar faces of my friends. Not finding them, I hunted for a pay phone. The instructions, written in Chinese, were no help in dialing my friends. A kind passerby showed me how the phone worked and offered me a coin. When I finally reached my friends, they apologized that they were unable to meet me but said they had booked me into a guesthouse in the New Territories. I jotted down the address.

I hailed the first taxi that came by. When I showed him the address, his foot pushed the gas, and the taxi shot forward along the crowded highway. After half an hour we had left the neon-lit city behind and were heading into the darkness of the New Territories. After a while the driver looked at me and asked to see the address.

"This no help," the taxi driver muttered in broken English.

"All I have is the address on this paper." I pointed to the crumbled paper with the address on it.

"I not know where place is!" the man exclaimed, his voice rising. "You get out!"

Get out here?—in the dark, in the middle of the undeveloped New Territories of Hong Kong? I did not relish the thought. Also, I suspected that the driver's order violated the regulations of the taxi company. I prayed under my breath. "Please Jesus, help!" Then turning to the irate driver, I pleaded, "Can't you just continue on for a bit more?"

Grudgingly he agreed. After driving a short distance I caught a glimpse of a woman dressed in a sari walking along the road. "Pull over," I instructed the driver. Rolling down my window, I showed the paper to the woman and asked if she knew the whereabouts of the address.

She smiled. "Why, that is where I am staying. Come and follow me, it is not far." Hastily, I pulled my traveling backpack from the taxi's trunk, paid my fare, and with a grateful heart followed the woman up a winding path. She led me to a small guesthouse. She apologized that the guesthouse manager had already retired for the night. Since I was expected, however, my room number should be posted on the whiteboard and my key in the clean room. Together we climbed the narrow staircase and discovered the room to be just as she had said. Relieved, I threw my backpack, fanny pack, and money belt on the bed. It felt good to be relieved of their load. Then I went down to see the kind lady to the door, as she would need to make her way to another building where her lodgings were.

As I returned to my room, I gasped. I had not taken the key and the door had locked when I closed it. Now what was I to do? I searched for someone who could help. One older woman remained awake. "I am sorry," she mumbled. "We can't get your key tonight. You'll have to wait till tomorrow. The room next to yours was vacated today. Let me see if it is still open." She pushed and the door opened. Soiled bed sheets still covered the bed. "Will this do for the night?"

I nodded.

"The bathroom is down the hall," she informed me before leaving.

I flopped onto the bed. Had God abandoned me? Why had He allowed this to happen? All through the past three weeks, He had so clearly gone before me. Now the situation did not meet my expectations. In frustration and exhaustion, tears trickled down my cheeks.

Then from deep within the recesses of my heart came that familiar voice, "Karen, will you accept the good from me, but not the bad? These past three weeks you have experienced my abundant blessings. Now they are temporarily removed from you. Am I alone enough for you? Emptied of your comfort and material blessings, am I enough for you?"

Without waiting long to reflect on the answer, my heart replied, "Yes, Lord. You are enough. You and You alone are my All-Sufficiency."

Rat-a-tat-tat.

"Who's there?"

"It's us."

The sound of the familiar voices brought joy to the old man under house arrest who had only seen the four walls of his room for the past year. Eagerly, he opened the door to welcome in the two young men. Tears flowed down their cheeks as they embraced one another.

"Oh Father! How thin and pale you have become!" the younger of the two exclaimed.

"God's grace is sufficient," the old man responded, lifting his face upward. "I have had such sweet times with God in this room, that I would not change it for the world."

"You mean you would not want to be free again?" asked the youth incredulously.

"Not if it meant losing this sweet fellowship with the Godhead which I now enjoy. God never takes something physical away from us without repaying us in spiritual dividends. Now I can truly say, to me to live is Christ, to die is gain.[19] Oh, to be forever with our dear Lord!"

The two younger men exchanged looks. They knew the older man meant what he said. They had lived with him long

---

19   Php 1:21.

enough to know that He truly cared about nothing else in this life except to know Christ more and more and to introduce others to the sweet fellowship that they, too, could have with Christ.

They looked around the bare room. They observed the blanket on the floor which served as their elder's bed. The sole furniture in the room consisted of a desk with a candle and candlestick holder, and a half-broken chair. The men could picture their spiritual father writing numerous letters of encouragement to the churches from this place.

The older of the two clasped the old mans hand. "Father, I am so glad to be here."

"I am so glad you have come, my son. I feel in my spirit that my days on this earth are numbered. I so desired to tell you once again that it is all worth the cost."

"Worth the cost?"

"Yes, worth the cost to know Him, worth the cost to serve Him. Everything else will be taken from us. Our purses, our houses, even the people we love. Only He cannot be taken from us. Invest in your relationship with Him, my sons. Make time for Him. Your ministry will flow out of the time you spend with Him. Let Him be your all in all."

The younger man's eyes glistened. The care of the churches often chipped away the time that he used to spend with the Lord. His early-morning renewal times with the Lord had slipped away almost completely. Instead he lifted up hasty prayers toward heaven and then raced to meet the demands of the day. His ministry to the churches lacked the power he had felt when the older man had been present. He attributed it to the fact that he just didn't have the same gifts as the older man. Now, however, as he again sat in the presence of this man who had taught and mentored him, he knew without asking that he, too, could serve the way the elder did, if he invested time in being with the Lord.

He bowed his head.

The older man asked gently, "You have let Him take second place to the ministry He has given you, haven't you?"

The young man nodded.

"So many fine apostles and disciples come to ruin in this way, my son. It all looks fine on the outside for a while. However, without timber the fire will burn out. Stoke the fire, my son. Don't let anyone or anything replace that time you spend with Him. He is worth it. Ministry will come and go. Successes will come and go. People will come and go. He will always be there. He is jealous for your affection. Draw near to Him and He will draw near to you."[20]

"May I pray for you two men?" the elder asked.

The two bowed their heads in assent.

Then lifting his head and hands toward heaven the elder's voice thundered, "Let these two men be filled with a passion for you, Lord, that they too would make it their earthly goal to know You. May their sufficiency not lie in what their hands can make or do, but rather in You and in You alone. Amen."

"Amen," came the echo.

Read: Acts 28:30–31, Philippians. 3:7–11, 2 Timothy 4:9–22

---

20   Jas 4:8 (NKJV).

My Sufficiency:
The one who is able to meet all my needs so that
I do not need to look elsewhere.

9

My Abba Father

"Come quick!" My mother's voice reached my ears.

I rushed out of the crowded office where I had been ordering an ambulance for my father and raced back to the small observation room where I had left my father and mother minutes before.

My father lay motionless on the cool clinic's floor with my mother sitting beside him. "He's not breathing. He has no pulse," my mother whispered.

Hastily, I urged a nurse in the hallway to call the doctor. I returned to my mother's side and felt for my father's pulse. Nothing.

The doctor entered. His face paled as he took in the sight. Since he was practicing a newer medical technique, sometimes criticized by the mainstream medical professionals, he feared any publicity which a scene like this could create. His low voice made the pronouncement we all knew in our hearts, "He is dead."

The ambulance attendants arrived and left. Since a medical practitioner had already pronounced my father dead, they could not take his body back to our town, an hour's drive away. Again I returned to the crowded office ... this time to call the undertaker.

My mother and I knelt by my father's lifeless body. Tears cascaded down our cheeks.

Only the day before, as I drove my car into my hometown, my Heavenly Father had asked me some heart-searching questions. "Do you believe that nothing can separate you from my love?"

"Yes," I replied.

"Do you believe that neither height nor depth, things present nor things to come, can separate you from my love?"

"Yes."

Now, as I sat in this sterile room, these words flooded back to my memory. Even at times like this, I was confident of my Heavenly Father's love.

Suddenly a thought flashed into my mind. "If you will thank me even for this, your time of grieving will be much easier." Hesitantly, I lifted my eyes to my mother's tear-stained face. "Mom," I whispered, "I know this may sound strange at such a time, but ... do you think we can thank God right now?"

As the tears flowed we clasped our hands over my father's cooling body and lifted up our voices in thanksgiving to the only father and husband that we knew would never leave us or forsake us. Our voices ascended to Him and His peace descended upon us.

That day as we followed the hearse with my father's mortal shell inside it, my mother and I sang songs of praise. His peace reigned in our hearts.

That is our Abba Father. He has promised to be a father to the fatherless and a defender of widows.[21] What we lack on this earth, He has promised to make up to us in the spiritual. If we welcome Him into our circumstances and obey Him even when it seems crazy to do so, He responds with the supernatural.

Although only three months remained from my father's passing until my wedding day, those months were filled with the knowledge and presence of my Abba Father's love.

So often in the Bible we read of the Father's love and the special care He gives to the fatherless. For many of us who have lost fathers through death or perhaps through emotional detachment, God's Father love can be made real to us as we cry out to Him from the deepest recesses of our hearts. He is for us. He answers our heart's cries.

Years ago, the Lord challenged me to "cry out to Him." He gently chided me that I would talk with Him and say "polite prayers" to Him but rarely did I cry out to Him. It is those cries that stir His heart to respond.

After I married, I actually grieved the loss of that sense of utter dependency I had felt with my Abba Father. When my husband took over my covering and protection, that supernatural closeness of God to the fatherless I had felt after my earthly father's passing dissipated. Those brief three months reinforced by experience that what we lack in the physical, God does supernaturally provide through the spiritual; so that we can say with Paul, "He has given us everything we need for life

---

21   Ps 68:5.

and godliness." [22] God never takes away without being available Himself to take up the slack.

With joy, the lad wrapped the new robe around his olive-skinned body. Every year when his parents came to the house of the Lord for their annual sacrifice, his mother presented him with a new cloak. With great pride he wore this garment, for it represented their love for him.

When they embraced and exchanged goodbyes, he swallowed hard to prevent his emotion from bursting forth. He loved them but he knew that he had been committed to a different way of life.

His world was in the sanctuary. The smell of blood and fragrant offerings; the sound of bleating sheep and cooing pigeons and the sights of dripping blood and grateful people were all common to his senses. The aging priest, with his bulging stomach and diminishing eyesight, often beckoned him to assist him in ministering before the Lord. He seemed to prefer the lad's swift obedience to his own sons' persistent rebellion. His grown offspring often forcefully grabbed the best meat from the worshipers for themselves, and they slept with the women who served at the entrance to the Tent of Meeting. They consistently ignored their father's pleas to repent.

The boy wearing the linen ephod, however, would sleep next to the ark of God. He loved that place, for he could sense the warmth of God there. It was almost like the strength and protection of a good father's presence.

---

22   2Pt 1:3.

Sometimes, though, as the boy crawled onto his mat at the close of the day, he would long for someone to talk with, someone who would be that father figure to him. He yearned for a father's voice to guide and direct him in the way to go. The old priest seemed too distant and too distracted with his own affairs to fulfill that role in his life.

Then one day it happened. Just as he was settling down to sleep, he heard a voice call his name. At first he assumed it was the priest's voice. When he raced to where the old man lay, the man informed him that it was not his voice he had heard.

However, again as he nuzzled his head into his pillow, he heard the voice. Again he tore into the next-door room only to hear the priest say that he had not called him. After it happened a third time, the wise priest suddenly realized who was calling the boy and he instructed him to lie down again. This time, however, when he heard the voice call his name, he was to respond with, "Speak, for your servant is listening."[23]

In eager anticipation, the lad lay down once more. The voice did not fail to call out his name again. This time the boy was prepared with an answer, "Speak, for your servant is listening."

As the boy grew to manhood, the voice which he first heard that night, became very familiar to him. He recognized the voice as that of the Father of his ancestors, Abraham, Isaac and Jacob. The voice could speak into situations and dispel the confusion. It could provide the guidance which he so longed for. The voice carried authority with it. It was the voice of the father he so craved—the Father that could put everything right; the Father who would not just visit him once a year but would always be there for him and had a greater purpose for him than

---

23   1Sa 3:9.

that which his physical father had. This was his Abba Father, with whom he could abide all the days of his life.

Read: 1 Samuel 1-3

⟫◦⟪

The True Father:
He not only creates the outer man but has the ability to call the inner man into being.
The voice of the Father, which once brought light into the greatest physical darkness, has the ability to bring light into our darkest moments of the soul.

⟫◦⟪

10

My Intercessor

I shuddered as I surveyed the filthy room with dirty syringes scattered on the hardwood floor and bird droppings lining the inside of the linen closet. I grabbed my husband's hand and whispered, "Let's get out of this place."

As we followed the manager of the rental unit down the broken concrete steps, I heard a familiar voice speak into my heart, "Do you not care that Sunnyville Community has more than a thousand and two hundred people who cannot tell their right hand from their left?"[24]

My heart sighed in resignation. I knew that Sunnyville, a government community housing project, would be our next home.

Within a few weeks, my husband, our infant son, and I moved our meager belongings into the three-story townhouse and started to acquaint ourselves with our neighbors.

---

24   Jnh 4:11.

Patti had five children, a few of whom were in and out of foster care because of her inability to provide for them. Her two youngest children struggled in school because of deficiencies at birth due to their mother's alcoholism. Patti's husband had just moved back in with her after a year's separation. Patti's life seemed to be one crisis after another. Despite our different cultures, we became friends.

Julie was pregnant with her second child from her common-law husband. Her future loomed uncertainly. Common needs of motherhood drew us together.

People in the community were not "projects" to us. They were friends.

One day a large local church initiated an outreach to the needy in our area. A pastor from the church encouraged me to come along to support the people with whom we had developed a relationship. Patti, Julie, and I entered the huge gymnasium where free manicures and haircuts were offered. I quite enjoyed the day until one lady mistakenly assumed that I was "one of them." My pride rose to the surface. I attempted to escape this undesirable identity. Then across my mind flashed the words, "He was numbered with the transgressors."[25] If Christ, in order to earn the right to intercede for us, was numbered with the transgressors, should I not have been willing to follow his example?

I returned home that day, humbled but honored that Christ had invited me to tread the road that He had trod. How can we truly intercede if we are not willing to identify with those for whom we are called to serve?

---

25   Isa 53:12.

With glowing face, the nimble, aged man descended the mountain. He reverently carried two stone tablets. His aide scrambled over the rocks to keep pace with him. Suddenly, the younger man stopped and exclaimed, "There is the sound of war in the camp."[26]

The older halted to listen. "It is not the sound of victory. It is not the sound of defeat; it is the sound of singing that I hear."[27]

As the two continued, the music grew louder. Their speed increased. What would cause such a commotion in the camp?

Suddenly the older stopped dead in his tracks. His face grew flushed, but not from his exertion. His anger burned. There before his eyes was a golden calf around which the people were parading. Some were prostrating themselves before it in worship.

How could this be so? Only forty days earlier the people had pledged themselves to follow the one true God. Only a few months earlier they had all marched through the Red Sea on dry land while God held back the waters. How could the people be so fickle as to abandon their faith so quickly upon a slight delay in his return? Could they not wait for God to act? Did they have to try to control situations themselves? Were they so fearful of the awesomeness of God, that they had to make a god they could manage? As these thoughts flooded his

---

26   Ex 32:17.
27   Ex 32:18.

mind, the aged leader lifted the two stone tablets high above his head and threw them in anger to the ground.

With this, the wild frenzy came to a halt. People retreated in fear.

The older man now could not be stopped. He grabbed the calf they had made and burned it in the fire; then he ground it to powder, scattered it on the water, and forced the people to drink the water.

In defense of God's name, the leader called those who were for God to come to him. One whole tribe rallied to him. He commanded them to strap a sword to their sides and march through the camp, killing those who were against God, whether they were brothers, friends, or neighbors. Three thousand people died that day.

As a result of their loyalty to God, this tribe was blessed and set apart to God.

The following day, the grieved leader again spoke to the congregation. "You have committed a great sin. But now I will go up to the Lord; perhaps I can make atonement for your sin."

Again the old man trudged back up the mountain. His heart was heavy with sorrow for the people that God had entrusted to his care.

Entering again into God's presence, he fell to his knees, "Oh, what a great sin these people have committed! They have made themselves gods of gold. But please," he pleaded, "Forgive their sin—but if not, then ... " The leader hesitated for a moment as he counted the cost of what he was prepared to say next. "But if not, then blot me out of the book you have written."[28] Although he himself had not sinned, these were his

28   Ex 32:31,32.

people, and the people that he was called to lead; therefore he was willing for their sin to be counted as his sin.

He prostrated himself before God Almighty's presence, awaiting the verdict, not just for the people but for himself as their true intercessor.

Read: Exodus 32:1-32

An Intercessor:
One not only willing to pray, but willing to identify with the people whom God has called him to stand in the gap for.

11

My Good Shepherd

The insistent high-pitched cries of my three-week-old son signaled his need to nurse. Drying my hands on an already damp towel, I turned my back on the stack of dirty dishes scattered over the kitchen counter. I pushed my Bible and notebook aside to make room for my still heavier-than-normal frame on the sagging couch. Reaching for little Samuel, I gently pulled him to me. My one-and-a-half-year-old had already dumped the box of toys on the floor beside me and was making boyish car sounds; my three-year-old, book in hand, crawled up beside me, no doubt hoping that I would read him a story. My husband, was out fixing the car again. I sighed. I knew this was a picture foretelling what the next three years of my life would be like.

Psalm 113:9 mentions "the happy mother of children." Sometimes I felt anything but happy. The endless diaper changes, sleepless nights, and, for us as overseas workers, the lack of routine.

We knew that God had called us to the life of pilgrimage for the sake of expanding His kingdom and we willingly had put our hands to the plow,[29] but now that we had three tiny ones depending upon us, we were more than ever in need of His grace.

I stared at the big windows with their blue- and white-striped curtains, the worn sofas and rugs, the coffee tables littered with books and tea cups. We were so thankful for this cottage-like home which our pastor and his wife had allowed us to use over the summer. But in two weeks, they would return and take their rightful occupancy. We would move to our fourth house of the year.

This time we would move in with My husband's recently widowed mother. We desired to be a blessing and not a burden, but how does one do that with three little ones in tow?

Suddenly the feelings of inadequacy stormed down upon me. I recalled how three years earlier, with our first son, I had tried to follow a popular Christian teaching on how to raise a child. I had failed. I could not live up to those requirements. The longest our family had any semblance of routine before a major move seemed to be three months. Since we were missionaries, I sometimes suspected that our supporters unconsciously required us to be the "perfect" parents. I knew I did not measure up. I felt that many other women were much better moms than I was, but I would keep trying. I would keep striving, I promised myself. Just thinking about it, however, made me feel exhausted. "Lord, how can I face another three years like this?" my heart cried out.

---

29   Lk 9:62.

"You do not need to be the perfect mom."

The Lord's response came like a spring bubbling up to sun-parched ground. My shoulders and body relaxed as they absorbed what the Lord's words meant. I could just enjoy being a mother, without the stress of having to be the perfect mom. I could be free to make mistakes and learn from them. My kids did not have to be perfect kids. My heart began to sing. Perhaps I could enjoy being a mom after all.

The Lord reminded me of the promise He had given for all mothers of young children in Psalm 113:9: "I will gently lead those who have young." I took comfort that God would be gentle with me. He would not condemn. Also, He would lead. My role, like a mother sheep, was just to follow the shepherd. As I followed the shepherd, my lambs, during the early years of their lives, would naturally follow behind.

The mother tried desperately to hold back the tears. She must be strong for the sake of her sons. Losing her husband only six months earlier had been hard for all of them. Having their creditors daily knocking on their door, demanding to be repaid, added greatly to her stress.

Now as she looked around her house, she knew that they had nothing more to give the creditors. Only a few drops of oil remained. Creditors had already taken everything they had. All that remained was her sons. She fought to gain control over her fears. She knew the law allowed creditors to enslave children until their debts were paid. She shivered in spite of the heat of the afternoon sun.

Memories flashed across her mind from the boys' childhood days. They had never been wealthy but they had always had enough. Her husband had been a man of faith. He had taught them to take every need to God in prayer. God had provided. Now with her husband gone, her own faith was being tested. Would God still provide for them? Did God really care about her sons and her?

Suddenly an insistent knocking at the door interrupted her thoughts. With trepidation she slowly opened the door. Was this the end?

Instead of the demanding stance of a creditor, the excited gestures of the wife of another prophet greeted her. "The man of God has come."

Without stopping to close the door, the woman followed her friend down the dusty road. "Where is he?"

"He is resting under the huge sycamore tree. I will take you there."

Oblivious to the stares that the sight of two grown women racing through the streets in the heat of the midday sun caused, the women pressed on.

Finally they came upon the respected prophet. At this point the kind neighbor took leave of her. Falling down at the older man's feet, the widow did not wait for an invitation to speak; her words tumbled out. "Your servant, my husband is dead, and you know that he revered the Lord. But now his creditors are coming to take my two boys as his slaves."[30]

The man of God wasted no words. "How can I help you? Tell me, what do you have in your house?"[31]

"Only a few drops of oil."

---

30   2Ki 4:1.
31   2Ki 4:2.

"Go around and ask all your neighbors for empty jars. Get as many as you can. Then go inside your house and close the door. Take what little oil you have and pour it into all the jars. As each one is filled, put it to one side."[32]

With eagerness, the woman hurried back to her house. She instructed her sons, "Go and ask our neighbors for jars."

Soon their little house was filled with jars. Then according to the prophet's words, the woman shut the door and started pouring the oil. Her sons removed the filled pots and brought the empty ones. "Bring me another one, and another," the woman continually repeated.

"Mother, they are all filled," her son finally announced. Then just as miraculously as it had started, the oil stopped flowing. The woman gazed around the room at all the filled pots of oil. The money that they would sell for equaled more than she could have ever imagined. They could pay off their creditors.

The woman, in gratitude, grabbed her two sons' hands and knelt down. She lifted up her face to her Heavenly Father. Quoting David's words, she said: "'You are indeed my Shepherd, I shall not want.'[33] Thank you, thank you for saving my sons."

Reading: 2 Kings 4:1–7

---

32   2Ki 4:4.
33   Ps 23:1.

The Good Shepherd:
The one who completely understands his sheep and gently guides them to green pastures.

12

My Protector

"Sorry, we have no more apartments available," the rental housing service agent apologized. "You will have to come back another day."

"But we don't have another day," my Chinese friend explained. "We already bought our bus tickets for tomorrow morning."

The man shrugged. He cared little about our dilemma.

My friend and I started to make our way out of the office. We had originally planned the trip to this city as a prayer journey. However, just before leaving our home, my husband had requested that I also look for housing as we planned to move down to this city in two months' time. Maintaing prayer as a priority, we had saved the last part of our final afternoon to look for housing. Now the housing office was about to close and the two apartments they had shown us lacked basic bathroom and kitchen facilities. "God, we honored you by putting you first, now please take care of our needs."

"Oh, wait," called the man from the desk. "Here is one more apartment. I'll try to contact the landlord for you."

Turning back into the messy room, my friend and I waited while he made the call. "Sorry, I couldn't get in touch with him. I'll try again later and give him your number."

My friend and I again headed for the door and slowly trudged back to our hotel room. Again we found our familiar places beside the bed, and lifted up our voices to our Abba Father. After an hour, we had almost despaired of hearing any word, when the phone rang. The housing agent told us to hurry as the landlord had already been waiting a long time for us.

We raced out of the hotel and up the block to where the disgruntled landlord stood. "I've been waiting an hour for you! Now I have no time to show you the apartment as I have another appointment." Again I whispered an S-O-S to my Heavenly Father as my friend tried to persuade the man. Finally he consented to call his wife to take us.

Within minutes we were rushing to keep up with his wife as she led us to an older block of apartment buildings. "Does the apartment have security?" I asked as we passed through a darkened alleyway.

"No," she mumbled.

Suddenly my interest in the apartment plummeted. Out of respect for the time she had taken to show us the place, we continued to follow her. Climbing up six flights of stairs, we reached the top and looked out the stairwell window to the busy courtyard below. Suddenly, a voice which I had come to know all too well, spoke into my heart. "I will be your fore guard and your rearguard." [34]

I knew at once that this apartment would be our next home, for our Lord does not waste His words. When we entered, I gazed around me. The ninety-seven square meter space allowed sunlight to enter through its relatively small windows. The large kitchen, which overlooked a busy street, would be adequate for our family of five. The kitchen sink however, had no drainage apart from a pail which stood under it. The washroom contained a dirty little squat toilet with no bathtub, just a pipe from the ceiling to act as a shower. The electrical wiring lay visible along the baseboard, a sure safety hazard for our three little boys, all under five years of age. However, I knew that I could make do. With a few minor renovations, this place would become home. That day, we informed the owner that we would take it. She warmly welcomed us to her home for dinner and we chatted about the history of the city.

Within two months, our little family moved in. That place became a meeting place for many in the community. Never once did we worry about security. Had the Lord not promised that He would be our fore guard and rearguard?

"How can you take so many people and so much gold on such a long unguarded road and *not* get robbed?" one of the people's elders questioned the organizer of the journey back to Jerusalem.

"I know it seems foolish, but we must depend solely upon our God's protection. I have already told the king that God will

---

34   Isa 52:12.

protect us. Now if I go back to him and ask for his cavalry to protect us, I am afraid that he may think that our God is not strong enough to protect us."

"Humph! I have never heard of such foolishness. Nevertheless, you are the leader; so have it your way."

"I plan to ask all the people to fast and plead to God to give us a safe passage. Without God's help, I know we are doomed. But, if God is for us, who can be against us?"[35]

"Well, we shall see what will happen. For now I will take my leave of you and attend to my own preparations."

As his companion walked out of his tent, the leader fell prostrate on the ground in the direction of Jerusalem. "Lord God of Israel, help us! I say with David of old, 'Some trust in chariots and some in horses, but we trust in the name of the Lord our God.'[36] Allow the people's hearts to join my heart in this fast." With that he arose and washed his face.

When he stepped out of his tent into the morning light, he could see that already masses of people had gathered on the plains to listen to his further instructions. As people caught sight of his white robe, a hush fell over the crowd. They held him in respect as a man of God who was well versed in the law. He knew, however, that he stood before them not because of his great learning but because the Lord had called him to lead the remnant back to Jerusalem and back to God, Himself.

"Beloved and chosen of God," his voice rang out across the thousands of people, "we make this journey because God has called each one here to make it. Since God has called, God will protect. We will not turn to the arm of man for protection but to the arm of God. I am calling you each to a fast. Petition God to give us a safe and smooth journey back to the land He

---

35   Ro 8:31.
36   Ps 20:7.

promised our forefathers. In three days we will leave. At the time of departure we will weigh out all the silver and gold which the king and his officials have donated for the house of God.

Let us be faithful now in prayer, to ask God to be our rear and fore guard."

"We will do as you have said," the people responded as one.

Their leader thanked God for the answered prayer of the people's support. He knew that the prophets of old, although they had heard clearly from God, rarely received the people's support. He concluded that the time in captivity had indeed softened the people's hearts. For this he was grateful.

Finally on the twelfth day of the first month, the multitude set out for Jerusalem. Excitement fluttered through the crowds. This seemed like a dream come true, to return to their homeland. After the Levites and priests had received the sacred gold and silver articles, and one final corporate prayer had been uttered, the group set out.

The journey, although long, passed quickly in the people's excitement at returning home. Upon setting foot upon the desired land of Jerusalem, the leader ordered a three-day rest. Then on the fourth day after their return, the leaders and priests gathered in the house of God to again weigh out the silver and gold. The scribes recorded another testimony of God's faithful protection: everything was accounted for by number and weight. In gratitude, the great assembly offered the God of Israel twelve bulls, ninety-six rams, and seventy-seven male lambs. With tears and outstretched arms they thanked their God who had never forsaken them. He was and ever would be their Great Protector.

Bible Reading: Ezra 8

Protector:
The one who is able to protect from all evil and all harm.

13

My Boss

"It is finished!" our friend Yvonne announced triumphantly.

I clapped my hands with glee. Eight long months of visiting government department after government department lay behind us. We now were officially registered as an independent foreign-run business.

"I'll tell you something," Yvonne confided, leaning slightly over the table. "I never believed you could pass through all those departments and obtain their approval without relying on higher-up connections."

"Oh but we did have a higher-up connection," I laughed, pointing heavenward.

"I know," Yvonne—also a sister in Christ—acknowledged. "But I have never seen anyone here in this Asian country get a job done without relying on connections. One time when it appeared that the police department would not give their approval, I was about to call a friend of mine for inside connections, but God stopped me. He reminded me that He was in control. Then after a few days the police department called us and told us we could pick up the papers we needed. I know now that even here things can be done by going through the front door instead of the back door if God is on your side."

We thanked God together. Little did I know that this small victory only represented the beginning of relying upon God in doing business.

To hire staff for our small cafe and guesthouse, we had turned to friends for help. Five young gals with whom we had developed friendships willingly agreed to assist in the kitchen. I anticipated no problems since we all enjoyed each others' company.

Within three months of our opening, however, I longed to resign as "boss." I hated telling others what to do. I disliked their looks of disapproval when they disagreed with a decision I'd made. I struggled to live with the constant gossip I knew existed in the same building in which we all lived and worked.

Unfortunately, the pressures of opening a business and training staff left little time to step back to regain perspective. For the first year we struggled on. Then—because God's timing is perfect—we were scheduled to take our year home-assignment leave. We eagerly departed, leaving the business responsibilities in the hands of a local Christian couple who had come on staff after our first set of staff had all resigned.

Even after half a year back in Canada, I had no desire to return to the guesthouse when we returned to Asia, but I had no choice. I knew that a lot of garbage had piled up in my heart during that brief period of being the boss. It needed dealing with or I would become a stinking aroma instead of the sweet aroma of Christ. With this knowledge, during our last few months in Canada, I signed up for a large Christian conference where I could remain anonymous.

There at the conference God met me. As the worship music played, God confronted me with my incomplete forgiveness towards the previous staff, myself, and Him. He quickly dealt with the first two categories. Then He revealed that I had not forgiven Him for asking us to open the business. "Karen," He chided, "you have never accepted the role of a boss as coming from my hand. You have continually rejected the boss's hat."

"I never asked to be boss," I retorted. "I just want to be the gals' friend."

"Karen, I am asking you to be boss."

"But Lord, it is too hard for me. I don't always make good decisions. My Chinese isn't that good and our staff do not speak English. The responsibility is too great."

"Karen," He responded gently, "I will be the senior boss and you will be the junior boss. Every decision you can run by me first. I will carry the greater weight for the cafe and guesthouse."

All of a sudden my burden vanished. I knew that the weight of the responsibility no longer rested with me. He was *my* boss. I would take my orders from Him and simply pass them on to the staff working for us. Ah, the air became so much easier to breathe again.

As their leader called out, "Return, O LORD, to the countless thousands of Israel,"[37] the men carefully set the ark down.

This invitation signaled that camp could be set up. People bustled about setting up tents, filling water jars, and making fires. No one seemed to be idle.

---

37   Nu 10:36.

However, as darkness set in, discontentment also seemed to creep in. The voices from each family's tent entrance could be heard. "We want meat! We want meat!"

Those closest to their leader's tent could be heard bemoaning ever leaving the land of Egypt. "We remember the fish we ate in Egypt at no cost, also the cucumbers, melons, leeks, onions, and garlic. But now we have lost our appetite; we never see anything but this manna!" [38]

Their leader's heart sometimes longed for the quietness he had experienced while shepherding four-legged sheep. These two-legged "sheep" always complained, it seemed. Today his own heart groaned before the only one He knew would listen to him. "Why have you brought this trouble on me, Lord? What have I done to displease you that you put the burden of all these people on me? Did I conceive all these people? Did I give them birth? Why do you tell me to carry them in my arms, as a nurse carries an infant, to the land you promised on oath to our forefathers?[39] I never applied for this job, Lord!"

With this, the bearded man sank to his knees. "Give me meat, they say! I cannot carry all these people by myself. The burden is too heavy for me."[40]

He waited for a response from God but there was none, so he continued his complaints.

"If this is how you are going to treat me, then put me to death right now and do not let me face my own ruin."[41] The man's body was racked with sobs. They were sobs resulting from the months of constantly standing firm in the face of opposition. First Pharaoh resisted his words and now the people

---

38   Nu 11:5,6.
39   Nu 11:11,12.
40   Nu 11:14.
41   Nu 11:15.

God had asked him to lead to the Promised Land seemed to balk every step of the way. Exhausted and discouraged, he lay before the one who had called him to this task.

God saw. God cared. God always cares about His servants. "Bring me seventy of Israel's elders who are known to you as Israel's leaders and officials among the people. Have them come to the Tent of Meeting with you. I will come and speak with you there, and I will take of the Spirit that is on you and put the Spirit on them. They will help you carry the burden of the people so that you will not need to carry it alone."[42]

Next God addressed the people's complaining. "Tell the people to consecrate themselves in preparation for tomorrow, when you will eat meat."[43]

"Eat meat?" The prostrate leader questioned. "Would there be enough if all the fish in the sea were caught for them?"

"Is the LORD's arm too short?" the LORD asked.[44]

The leader accepted the rebuke. He had witnessed God's faithfulness many times before. He knew that God was Israel's provider and leader. He was only the Almighty's servant and spokesperson.

As he rose to his feet, his heart felt lighter. He was not in charge. God was. That was a comforting thought. He took courage to again face the people God had given him to lead.

Scripture: Numbers 10:33–11:35.

---

42 Nu 11:16,17.
43 Nu 11:18.
44 Nu 11:22,23.

A Boss:
The one who gives orders and makes
the final decision.

14

My Sustainer

R-r-r-ing! The phone's persistent clanging interrupted my early-morning meditative thoughts.

"Wei," I gave the customary Chinese greeting.

"Karen, I have an urgent question I need to ask you. Could you come downstairs?"

Sighing inwardly, I agreed. Another busy day had begun.

Racing down the four flights of stairs to the cafe below, I found the young staff waiting for me.

"A relative just passed away," Sandra blurted out. "I need to go back to my hometown for a funeral. Can I have the weekend off?"

I could not refuse. Already short-staffed, I knew it meant that I would have to work in the kitchen over mealtimes on Saturday in addition to teaching six hours of English classes and leading two Bible study classes. I would also need to miss the foreigner's gathering on Sunday morning to assist in the kitchen.

Sandra then shared with me the circumstances surrounding the death. Together we prayed and looked to God for His grace in the situation. The majority of people where we lived had never heard the name of Jesus and only a few had committed their lives to Him. Death was not only the loss of a loved one for Sandra but the knowledge of her eternal separation from God.

After a quick hug for Sandra, I retraced my steps. My husband and sons had already finished breakfast. Looking at the clock I knew that I had no time to sit down and enjoy the delicious cinnamon buns which our staff had made. I had just enough time to grab a drinking yogurt and herd our three boys together to start their homeschooling.

At one o'clock Becky at the front desk, called up to inform us that lunch was served. We raced down and ate a simple Chinese lunch with the staff. We chatted about the news in the community and their lives. Sharon, our oldest staff member agonized over the amount of money a local high school required in extra fees for her daughter's education. Only occasionally were receipts issued for the money paid. No one, however, dared to confront the teacher or officials; if they did, their child would suffer the consequences. Our conversation ended abruptly upon the arrival of Sue, a young Korean gal.

Glancing at the clock, I knew that I must return to teaching. In the afternoons, Sue joined the boys in order to improve her listening comprehension in English. Before moving to our city, Sue had gone to an international school. Her Korean parents felt inadequate to help her improve her oral English so they welcomed the offer that she join our three boys in their afternoon classes. We all thoroughly enjoyed Sue's delightful personality. As three-thirty neared, I excused myself and let the children finish their assignments on their own.

Grabbing my bag, Annie, a young gal on staff, and I headed for the bus which would take us downtown to visit a local sister in the hospital. When we arrived there, we encountered the familiar scene of people mingling about. Not only did the patients live within the hospital's wall, but their family members, who bore the responsibility of providing food and basic care twenty-four hours a day, dwelt there too. If a sick person did not have a friend or relative who could take him to the washroom, get him a cup of water, or bring lunch in for him, he could hire an assistant—similar to a nurse's aid but with no formal training. Fortunately, our friend had a relative who could provide for her basic needs.

After an encouraging visit we boarded the bus again. I struggled to find a rung to hang on to. The people on their way home from work and school all pushed in till we were packed like sardines. Despite the invasion of personal space, however, I enjoyed the bus ride, for it allowed me to relax and pray for the city God had called us to.

Arriving home, I again trudged up the four flights of stairs. On the way, I bumped into Shona, our hearing-impaired helper. I gestured for her to follow me. Together we prepared dinner.

We had just sat down as a family to eat, when again the phone rang. This time a parent wished to see me downstairs. She wanted her son to register for our weekend English classes but had some questions she would like answered first. No, she said, she could not wait.

After answering her multitude of questions I returned to a cold dinner and empty chairs. The boys had run downstairs to play on the computer and my husband had an English class to teach.

I had barely finished my meal when the phone rang again, this time to inform me that an expected friend was waiting downstairs. Hurriedly clearing the table I awaited for this local sister's arrival. She had called earlier with something on her heart that she sought counsel for.

As I glanced at the clock and saw the hands nearing 8:30, I called the boys from the computer room to get ready for bed. Then I briefly excused myself to pray with them. Returning to my guest, we continued to talk long after the doors of the cafe had closed at 9:00. When finally I sensed that God had brought peace and clarity to her situation, I saw her off to a taxi and took our dog for a brief walk. Walking our dog late in the evening had become my husband's and my time to share and get caught up with each others' day. That night however, he was still talking with a student.

As I passed our staff's dorm door on the way upstairs, Lonnie, the youngest gal popped her head out. "Karen, my dad just called."

I could see that she was near tears.

"Can I talk with you?" Although I longed for bed, I knew that Lonnie did not often open up; I needed to be available when she was willing to talk.

"Sure," I responded. "Why don't we meet in the corner guestroom? There are no guests there now."

Not until nearly midnight did I crawl wearily into bed to complete another normal day of our lives at the guesthouse. I thanked God for His strength.

I would often recall an event which happened a few weeks before our guesthouse and cafe's grand opening. At the time we were in Thailand attending a conference sponsored by our sending organization. During the last morning, the participants all shared in communion together. Suddenly, as we were about to break bread, the enormity of the task at hand overwhelmed me. In addition to homeschooling and playing a key role in a young church, I would be running an English program, managing a cafe and acting as hostess at the guesthouse. I failed to restrain my tears. How could I ever carry such a load?

A sister, observing my emotional state, offered to pray for me. During her prayer I saw in my mind a picture of myself seated with Christ in the heavenly realms far above the guesthouse and all the work it entailed. Immediately my stress level decreased. God had revealed to me that if I remembered my position with Him in the heavenly realm, the stress of the work could not touch me.

During those four years, although we worked almost eighteen hours a day, we fervently held to our Sabbath Day of rest on Monday, the only day which the guesthouse was closed. That was our day to draw near to God and to each other as a family. Often we would cry out to God to lessen the load or send others to help, but His answer remained the same: "My grace is sufficient for you."[45]

We learned through this season that God indeed is our sustainer. He carried us through when we ourselves did not think we had the strength to face the next weekly challenge.

---

45   2Cor 12:9.

"What are those feeble Jews doing? Will they restore their wall? Can they bring the stones back to life from those heaps of rubble, burned as they are?"[46] The taunts of their advisory could be heard above the grinding of mortar and the chisel.

Another voice joined in, "What are they building? If even a fox climbed up on it, he would break down their wall of stones!"[47]

The leader of the work expedition turned aside so that the workers could not see the discouragement on his face. Walking away from the workers until he was hidden from view, he dropped to his knees amidst the rubble. "Hear us, O our God, for we are despised."[48] After pouring out his frustration and discouragement before the Lord, he waited to hear the Lord's response.

His waiting was rewarded. "My purposes cannot be thwarted. My purposes shall stand forever." The leader got to his feet. He knew that God would not let them see defeat. God would enable them to finish the task.

With a lighter step, he returned to his supervisory position. The people themselves, however, had not heard from God. Worry and fear remained rooted in their hearts. One whispered to another, "Our strength is giving out and there is so much rubble that I don't see how we can rebuild this wall."[49]

---

46   Ne 4:2.
47   Ne 4:3.
48   Ne 4:4.
49   Ne 4:10.

"Also," another added, "our enemies keep saying that they will come and kill us and put an end to our work. If they kill us, our wives and children will be unprotected. Perhaps they will take them as slaves."

Anxiety accented their weariness. Their efforts slowed and their output decreased significantly.

Finally, their leader addressed the situation. Gathering the people together, he instructed them to post guards at the lowest points of the walls. "Half of the men will do the work while the other half will be equipped with spears, shields, bows, and armor. Every man and his helper will stay inside Jerusalem at night so they can serve as guards by night and workmen by day."[50]

The people half-halfheartedly agreed to the plan. Their faces, however, remained plagued by fear.

Suddenly their leader realized that he needed to address that greater enemy of fear. "Don't be afraid of them!" he shouted. "Remember the Lord, who is great and awesome!"[51]

Then, as if by an invisible leading, the men one by one started to recount what God had done for them in the past. He had led them across the Red Sea. He had provided them with manna in the wilderness. He had helped them conquer the tribes of Canaan. He had granted their leader favor with the king, who had supplied them with the resources they needed to rebuild the wall. Finally, their hearts became convinced that God was indeed great and awesome. He indeed could protect them from the enemy.

Then their leader shouted, "Fight for your brothers, your sons and your daughters, your wives and your homes!"[52]

---

50   Ne 4:22.
51   Ne 4:14.
52   Ne 4:14.

Hearing these words, the men's protective instincts rose to the surface. Yes, they would fight. They would succeed; for God Himself, would sustain them. He would be their strength!

Read: Nehemiah 4

—◈—

My Sustainer:
The one who holds me up when
I feel like I'm crashing down.

—◈—

15

My Hope

Like many missionaries in their first year of language study, I struggled with my sense of identity. When I had taught English in the same country years earlier, people addressed me as a teacher. Now, although older and wiser, I was simply a language student in a new culture where no one knew my past accomplishments. At times I felt lost, not only within the culture, but within myself. Who was I? Did I matter to anyone, apart from my husband and son? Of course, as an adolescent, I had wrestled with these questions. What answer had I arrived at then? Did my grades, future career, peers, and church involvement then define who I was? Now these attributes were stripped away from me and I was forced to return to square one. Who really was, I anyway? What significance did my life hold?

For months, my insecurity raged, causing frustration within my marriage and discontentment with my place in life and society. One day, however, 1 John 3:1 caught my attention. It stated, "How great is the love the Father has lavished on us, that we should be called the children of God!" The words, "children of God" rang in my mind. That was who I was; I was simply a child of God! My root identity consisted in this alone. The knowledge of this truth brought an end to my striving in my marriage and in society. I knew who I was, I did not need to strive to prove myself anymore.

Years passed on the field. In addition to the roles of wife and mother I assumed many other roles: teacher, leader, intercessor, counselor, and so on. However, after years of being overseas, the time came for my family and I to return home for what is now called a "home assignment." Again, as I caught a glimpse of what that year might hold, my heart skipped a beat. No one would know me for who I had become or what I had done. I would lack identity again.

This time God graciously gave me a picture. He compared the different roles I filled to mantles I had worn. One by one He removed these mantles from me until none remained. All that remained was a young child. "Karen," He said tenderly, "this is who you are when you return to your home country. You are my child. That is the root of your identity. All other mantles will come and go and you must not cling to them. This identity I will never remove from you, it is yours to keep. Be secure in this calling, my child."

Suddenly the fear of again being a nobody disappeared and joy welled up in my heart. I was a child of the King and this inheritance could never be taken from me, for Christ was in me, the hope of glory.[53]

---

53   Col 1:27.

"Senior brother, how good to have you come and teach at our synagogue. I listened to you teach in a synagogue in Jerusalem years ago. Your rhetoric was outstanding. If I recall, you also had a long list of accomplishments which the leaders listed. Let's see if I remember some—"

"Please, you don't need to mention those."

"Oh, but it was quite impressive. Oh yes, I remember— you are from the tribe of Benjamin. What a great ancestry! The leaders also described you as being a very zealous and most promising Pharisee. One even declared that you were blameless in regard to the law. That's quite an achievement! Not many people receive that compliment. Well, tell me, at what synagogue do you regularly teach? How many disciples do you have? And if you don't mind me asking, what is your yearly income? I am sure it is quite a sum."

"Well, sir, none of that matters anymore. I am no longer seeking to be a great orator or to have a huge following."

"You're not? Why, what else could matter in life for one with your talent and ability?"

"That is just it, my young friend. I consider everything a loss compared to the surpassing greatness of knowing Christ Jesus, for whose sake I have lost all things. I consider them rubbish, that I may gain Christ."[54]

"Isn't that comparison a bit too strong? Think of how long you worked to gain the position you had. Surely your

---

54 Php 3:7.

position could glorify God and through it you could help many people."

"Like the psalmist, I would rather be a doorkeeper in the house of my God than dwell in the tents of the wicked."[55]

"What about dwelling in the tents of the righteous? Surely God would allow you to keep that position."

The older man looked at the younger man with sadness. He knew that "head" knowledge of the things of God could never replace that which came through revelation and experience. "My friend, God's way is often down—to the foot of the cross. Unless we are willing to humble ourselves and give up all, we can only receive from him a minute fraction of that which He is prepared to give us."

"But teacher, the fame and popularity which comes from rising in the esteem of the religious community—how can that be wrong?"

"Anything is wrong, if it eats away at our devotion to Christ. We cannot serve both God and men. We must choose whose affirmation we seek, men's or God's."

Silence swallowed the young man's thoughts for quite some time. Finally he spoke again. " How is the affirmation of God so much better than that of man?"

The elder softened at the childlike nature of the younger man's question; he had ceased pretending.

"Friend, men's esteem will come and go like grass blown by the wind. Sometimes it will rest at your side and other times it will be blown away. If you seek the praises of men, including those within the religious community, your heart will never be at rest. If you seek the favor of God, your heart can rest secure. He will become like an anchor for your soul."

---

55   Ps 84:10.

The younger man knew from experience the truth in the older man's words. For many years he had sought the approval of the rabbi he had chosen to follow, but always there were those younger and more capable who shone where he waned. His soul wearied of the endless search for approval. Could it be that he had looked in the wrong place?

As if reading the other's thoughts, the elder said, "Hope is not all lost. There is still time to shift your focus to Jesus, the author and perfecter of our salvation. He will provide that anchor and that affirmation you seek. Turn to him, my friend, and be satisfied. In Him is everything of value that you seek."

The young man embraced the older man's words. Kneeling beside the outer walls of the synagogue, he prayed, "Jesus, please be the anchor for my soul, my hope both now and forevermore."

The God in heaven who hears all prayers, answered him with a clash of thunder and a downpour of rain. As the two men sought refuge inside, they knew that they would eternally rest secure in the Almighty's arms of love.

Bible Reading: Philippians 3:1–11

Hope:
That which motivates us to keep going
in life.

Psalm 31:14
I trust in you, O LORD:
I say, "You are my God."